DREAMLINES

Jenny Johnson

Emoter's Gap

First published in Great Britain in 2021 by
Emoter's Gap, an imprint of Eskdale Publishing, North Yorkshire

Text copyright © Jenny Johnson, 2021
www.jennyjohnsondancerpoet.net

Cover and interior illustrations copyright © Antony Wootten, 2021
www.antonywootten.co.uk

A Catalogue record for this book is available from the British Library.
ISBN: 9798705088645

For my dear friend and fellow dreamer

Marilyn Hyde

Contents

Preface i

DREAMLINES 1

Dreamlines 3

Frances 5

On the Edge 6

War Zones 8

Felix 10

Ecovillage: Inner City 12

The Namesake 13

The Cluster 15

Out of Its Element, Nothing Can Flourish 17

Gawn 19

Baggage 20

Peculiar Corners 22

Who Needs a Script? 24

The Campus 26

A Sequence of Challenges 28

Monuments 30

The Guest 33

I Am Swift Purpose 35

The Drama Class 38

A Long Day 40

The Concert 42

Hair Power 45

The Crash..48

Make Believe 50

The Besom 53

Finding My Bearings..56

Maeve..59

Hoping for Venus..61

All or Nothing..63

From Sluggard to Hummingbird..65

Polarities 68

Hot Moon..70

Anaemia..72

Cartoon..74

Chagrin..77

1 Woller Gardens..79

The Promise..81

Bessie..83

A Fragile Blue 86

On the Road to Hope Cove 88

Facade 90

Acting Out..92

OCTET..**95**

Shanklin Rain..97

On the Other Side..98

Camaraderie in the Margins..100

The Host of the Holly 101

Tempest..102

Crouch 104

Not Knowing 105

Chiaroscuro 107

About Jenny Johnson **109**

Acknowledgements **111**

Preface

The *Dreamlines* sequence arose from my own dreams. Some years ago, I spent nearly a decade studying this surrealist world within a small group. We met twice yearly for an intensive weekend, which included the sharing of recent dreams. The facilitator was Madeleine O'Callaghan, who encouraged each participant to narrate her/his dream in the first person. The listeners responded, without interruption, by beginning with the words, "If this were my dream", and then pointing out which symbols, actions, characters etc. were important to them. There was no fixed interpretation of anything: for example, the sea might represent a healing force to one person and a severe threat to another. Madeleine often suggested that we create a drawing to express our emotional reactions – or that we dialogue with one of the symbols or characters. Once all the dreams had been narrated and explored, a common theme would frequently emerge – from which we all gained valuable insights…. I invite you to respond to my poems in a similar way.

You are welcome to visit my website, www.jennyjohnsondancerpoet.net, where you will find a sample of my published poems. *Octet* is mostly set in Exmouth, Devon. I find the sea very conducive to creativity.

Jenny Johnson

DREAMLINES

Dreamlines

I coast along the highway in my open-top jalopy:
a luxury forbidden in the otherlife –
where tests have been avoided.

Noon levitation begins in the abdomen:
poised above an orchard, I can dance to the rhythm of leaves.
In the otherlife, I am cast down at the very mention of heights:
even between my twin realms, limbs begin to stiffen.

I swim within the warmest sea – or at least breast an estuary:
in the otherlife, how intensely I bear with that sea –
unable to deal with the gravity of the moon, the sun!

I am done with trying to read street signs or dates in newspapers:
a dyslexic dance of the figure and the glyph sets me free.
Electricity goes crazy.

      *   *   *

When I am *sure* that I am dreaming, I prove it immediately
by pushing a right finger through my left hand:
the bloodless cavity closes up within seconds.

If I alter the colour of a ceiling, or the sky,
I am always reminded that spinning around fast
is the route to a new location.

How safe I feel when I move over the rooftops
and hover above the valley!
I coax all the crocodiles and lions with my lullabies.

Here, I am in rehearsal:
I practise drama after drama, night after night,
until I am fully attuned to whatever I sense ...

as I can be in the otherlife – now and again.

Frances

The longest dreams are the last ones.
Often, they turn into five act plays in which
I ad-lib continuously:
when their lines are set, I either ignore or forget them.
And nobody minds: I am usually applauded.

How I love you, my co-creator,
with your red-gold hair and green eyes!
You hold me so firmly in the cream of your arms:
you hide me so well from the widening of the pupil –
the inquisitive glance of an acquaintance or rogue.

       *   *   *

As five act play becomes televised film,
you are primed for the priesthood….
Strangely subdued, you devalue our *own* communion.
Your visions are abridged. Your belief in the infinite
leaves little room for the co-creator.

Unseeing, in front of a portrait window,
I sip the remains of your wine from stained glass….
Drying my cheeks, I look for the company of like-minded women:
my dream will be seen on the broadest of screens:
they will applaud.

On the Edge

Perimeter Girl, he calls me:
a role that I am reluctant to accept.
The rest of the cast is absorbed in its movements.
For once, it matters that I only ad-lib.
I feel like a clown
in my psychedelic poncho and my jabot.
I jab at the air with occasional nouns.

In the auditorium, my adoptive mother and father
are waiting to be satisfied.
This theatre has so many rooms on so many levels
that I lose my way entirely between scenes.
Costumes disappear, are borrowed or stolen:
in the second act, I approach bare-chested and bereft:
someone in the wings brings me a blanket.

                  *   *   *

After the performance, I escape to the wardrobe
to tug at my lacquered wig.

I can hear you in the foyer, Frances:
can hear the dramatist in you;
the argument with our director, Felix.
"But she's so enthusiastic!" you say of me.
"Tomorrow, her forgotten lines will be recollected,
her lost garments found."

As always, you have delved into my need to be centred.

Relieved, encouraged, I search for my chequered tabard
and for my copy of your script.

War Zones

A drone loiters to the north of me,
its presence as arresting as that of a tableau:
I move south.

A spherical weapon rises above the horizon,
zones right in,
glances off the adjacent wall:
I cower.

The falling bomb looks full of itself
till it fails to explode:
for a second, I am stilled.

Then over and over I turn to the left
till my fear can carry me no further:
till the region of the drone, the sphere, the bomb,
reappears.

       *   *   *

I come to myself in the grounds of a school:
its hedged field provides nothing more
than the briefest asylum.

Abrupt girls take it in turns to unsettle:
they hurtle me into the nettle beds
with unpunctuated taunts.

I limp indoors, am not surprised
when their classroom begins to drive off:
I concentrate on a windowpane, a passing leaf.

        *   *   *

Later, when I complain to the Head,
she ignores, then disbelieves:
threatens me with her electric prod.

I escape to the south, the west, the north,
yet whenever I look behind, there she is
with her thick lenses, her baton and gown.

Not yet conscious in my dream, I can only remain
trapped within its plot:
I hide in a hedge, in a cubicle.
Wait.

Felix

Felix is a man with a complex.
Often too loud, he has an unexpectedly
soft footfall. And hair that never goes gray.

His presence invites peril.
You tell me he is a womaniser, Frances,
but I feel your fascination for him.

He overwhelms with platter after platter of food,
most of which we cannot eat:
I secrete mine in my bag within a bag:
he pretends not to notice.

He offers to escort us into town, to upgrade his day.
"I need the restroom," I reply,
but neither of you knows where to find one.
"We will wait at the corner," Felix decides.

                *   *   *

An hour later,
I balance on a toilet seat, only to see
a burst of children spilling around me.

Furious at their trespass, I allow myself
to be led to a cave – where too many tourists
are jostling each other, hanging over its rails.
Queues are unheard of: passages are breathless.

Once outside, whom do I see but *you*, Frances,
lying face down in a shallow pool.

Afraid that you have fainted, might even have drowned,
how easily I pull you out by your auburn plait –
as though you were a cloth doll!
I ask in a nearby haberdasher's for a towel, a quilt.

When I venture to mention the name of Felix,
you fail to look me in the eye:
I go away.

Half conscious, I flow uphill, just above the traffic.
After a while, I conjure up an electric bicycle:
levitation is hard on the abdomen.

             *   *   *

Felix is in his café, busily ignoring my questions.
He steps aside: slips into his back yard.

I follow him: he refuses to countenance
yarns about a cave, a bicycle, a restroom.

Do you *need* to be at odds with Frances?" I ask.

His response – safer than a sigh –
is to bake me a soufflé.

Ecovillage: Inner City

The ravine in the village of my parents
is filling with trees:
their canopy is level with the pavements either side.

An avenue leads to the cluster on the border –
a community whose dream is of self-sufficiency;
whose medicine is grown in a garden.

I am welcomed by a woman who is bare-breasted
and oddly familiar:
her companions work the land wearing bamboo and hemp.

In a converted manor house, a velvet curtain shelters both
the dreamer on the stage and the dancer on the sprung floor:
nothing is wasted.

A minimum of water is used here;
meals are unmolested, raw….
Many of my friends have so easily assimilated.

I come and go; I make my way towards the innards of the city,
whose meals taste of its twelve o'clock dust….
Images from childhood are challenged, rearranged.

In the following lull,
I am suddenly aware of the Avon Gorge rising –
of an urgency in the sky.

The Namesake

Revisiting the village-become-suburb,
my childhood namesake and I begin
checking on our elders, on ourselves.

We allow our results to coil around each other....
Her graduate years have undoubtedly affected her:
sometimes, she sounds like a textbook.

I reacquaint her with my adoptive mother,
but she comes and goes unrecognised:
time has revised both forms and memories.

The last glimpse of my namesake is through a frosted pane –
until, decades later, I discover her on the platform
of the very hall where that checking and coiling took place.

I watch her through an exit's reinforced glass:
I call to her, embarrassed at pronouncing my own name:
she saunters towards me: the door is half open.

"You can find my details online," she informs me....
I feel unwell, then thoroughly erased:
clearly, she cannot – *will* not – place me at all.

A few of her hooded companions gather by the stage:
I join them: I wait with them in silence,
not knowing why.

One by one, they take their leave – and then I see her again,
high on a dais with a female partner:
age has honed her lower face; her hair gleams.

The Cluster

I stand at the door, afraid to go forward
into the February raw.
My possessions lie low in their turquoise case.
Much has been taken away, sold:
music for piccolo and oboe – all silvers and golds –
but none of my poems.

Panic makes me hollow:
where on the planet do I sleep tonight?
My adoptive parents have ordered me
to fend for myself: they cannot afford me any longer.
And I know they are right.

Frances, at last! You wind around one of my corners
and touch me gently on the shoulder.
You have found me a place in a cluster,
where I can listen to the infant and mind the adolescent.
It is one of a growing number.

The mother is full of sustenance and music:
she dances for my songbook;
sighs when I say I have given it away.
A girl with curly hair prepares my food:
fingers and thumbs are her cutlery.

As I fashion my bread into a spoon,
her brothers relax on the floor with their father.
"We have no religion, no politics," he says.
"Christ, Mohammed, the Buddha, is within:
we anoint ourselves with our own wine."

At this, a young man allows pink liquid
to spill onto my blouse. The larynx tightens.
"Look how it stains! Look at it!" I hiss.
"Often, there is beauty in a stain," he responds.
He anoints me with the remains of his juice….
Increasingly awake in my dream, I let go.

Out of Its Element, Nothing Can Flourish

Miles from any coast, the first family I meet
attempts to draw me into its high-ceilinged world:
a world of unopened windows.

I remember the town from previous dreams.
Would anyone but Felix propel me
into such desiccation?

When you bring me away in that pickup truck, Frances,
how unfazed you are by the number of vagrants
who jump on board!

Wanting my home, the ocean, I ask for the station….
There, behind sliding doors, are rail tracks
crossing each other at right angles.

Train spotters freeze: they gaze at those rails
until a grotesquery is upon us.
It cannot stop

for immediately afterwards, a giant clone bellows past:
I stare at twin gashes in the walls
through which it has burst.

A small boy wails. "They are trying to kill me!"
I gather him up, as much for my own consolation as his:
he feels boneless in my embrace.

It is cruel to remain here;
nevertheless, I am held against my will within
the immensity of it all.

When I next look down to check on the boy,
I find that I am cradling a terracotta pot.
In it, there are slivers of liver and kidney

which, once I am able to focus,
wriggle and diminish till they
disappear.

        *   *   *

Perhaps, if I had escaped earlier,
I could have saved him.
As it is, I am late for a civic reception.

When I arrive, it is you, Frances, who acknowledges
what Felix ignores.
"Out of its element, nothing can flourish," you declare.

Gawn

Gawn is my son.
In waking life, he is a man: in the dream, he is nine:
here, he exists with a host of others like him.

In a square room, parents perch on sand dunes
which, at less than a moment's notice, can be
stabilised by marram grass: vanished by sea.

Gawn fixes his gaze on me: it penetrates my guilt
at having given him away. How ironic it is
that he makes eye contact with nobody else.

A man, a woman, approach in turn and kneel down
to engage him: he speaks in a monotone,
continually tugs at his earlobes.

For a long time afterwards, he sulks on top of a cupboard.
"I want to build a bridge," he eventually mutters.
He descends and crouches by a model railway

to line up all the detached parts.
I sigh: a bridge is no metaphor to him.
But in a dream, it is just that, I remind myself.

Outside, I choose the causeway between opposing seas:
one a light turquoise with artificial waves,
the other more sombre – the colour of Gawn's eyes.

Baggage

Down by the stable-house, I can see how a spring tide
jumps over a limestone wall –
how it accelerates without its brakes.

Shall I rescue my belongings – poetry and jewellery,
homeopathic medicines and drapes?
Something within me hesitates.

My fingers are leaden: my mind is as fixed
as my sun sign, waterlogged Scorpio.
My pale green suitcase is nowhere to be seen.

I come to the end-of-term dinner-dance of a hillside school:
shivering in the kitchen, I plead for my food….
Leftovers are unheard of.

When I take my possessions to linoleum,
how slippery they are!
My hands are too numb to arrange or discard them.

Waltzing women breathe around me; they carry me
into an alcove. They dip and rise, dip and rise
till they carry me again.

In the linen room, whose floor is bare, my paraphernalia lies on
a silver salver. The pale green suitcase is nowhere to be seen.
"You have run out of time," an examiner complains.

She waits behind a counter, the salver in front of her.
"You will have to pay a fine to redeem them," she pronounces:
she fastens price tags to my garments, my poems.

I howl. I explain how unstable I have been –
how unable to take control, to recall.
I yell at her. "Where is my suitcase?"

A framed picture becomes her cupboard door.
She opens it wide. "There it is, your precious container!"
She refuses to hand it over.

"Thieving bully!" I accuse. "I shall tell the authorities."
She smiles with only her lips and disappears.
I try to believe she will never return.

At ebb tide, I claim my accoutrements with ease.
The silver salver is polished so well
that it challenges the eye.

Peculiar Corners

A trio of aeroplanes deafens both my heights
and my foundations: I can stand its vibrations no longer –
can imagine lesions in the brain.

Felix is unfazed. "It's a regular practice," he explains….
How relaxed you are, Frances, with your friends and paying guests!
"Any breakfast?" you ask me, an empty cereal bowl in your hands.

I am conscious that packing is to be done, that I am partially dressed.
In my confusion, I button cardigan over cardigan and hurry round the corner
to the baker's, as if buying a loaf might keep me in place.

When I return, I watch through the window how my son, Gawn,
shifts from fear to fear in the unfamiliar company of twins –
the bullies of the alley.

       *   *   *

I hurry round the corner, craving diversion in order to cope
with peculiarity. And when I return, everything is changed.
"Frances? Felix?" I call. Over and over.

Each room is a hospital ward, its light focused
on caramel walls and wounded patients.
Gawn, the twins, the paying guests and friends, are inaccessible.

A black cat tickles my cheek with a whisker:
after the ritual of stroking and purring,
she leaves with her tail held high. And I follow her.

Who Needs a Script?

Even in the cloakroom, I can hear the beginnings of a ritual
to invoke Gabriel; the creativity of July.

Entering the hall by its back door – encumbered
by my purple coat and rubber boots – I come upon

an oval of dancers loosening their arms and trunks
but with feet rooted to the parquet floor. Felix instructs.

Lateness makes me passive: I observe how the oval finds its toes
and turns into a round.

       *   *   *

Afterwards, on the coach home, Felix summons us, one by one,
to sit up front beside him, to give an account of ourselves.
I carry the plainest of exercise books. I know my lines.

In my suburb, it is Wendy – a friend with a pageboy haircut –
who tells me to climb onto her back
so that we can skim rooftops. The book plummets.

We continue for a day, Wendy and I – a time when fear of heights
is dissolved by reliance on her Aquarian element. Air….
As soon as we land, she evaporates.

In the aftermath, my chosen path is through woods
where, freed from Felix, I lament her absence for mile upon sleepy mile,
until the moment when a deep pool excludes me.

"This is our dream!" I inform the reflections. "Who needs a script?
Anything can happen: I can levitate over the likes of you."
And I do.

The Campus

Ages have passed since I first set foot on this campus:
I am eighteen going on seventy.
Today, without a timetable, I am unable to learn
the when and the where of my tutorials.
Unless I can find one, I will fail and be expelled.

In contrast, my namesake is established
and has a polished sense of timing and direction.
I weep for assistance; but she is taken up
with fellowships and grandsons.

As I wander from one end of the campus to the other,
I meet my nemesis-turned-friend, Rosalind.
Post-retirement, she is concerned with nothing less
than a toddler of a husband: I watch how versions of him
drape themselves over adapted cots.

        *   *   *

As a last resort, I approach a woman who styles herself
as the Vice-Chancellor's Caretaker.
I explain my desperation to her half-closed casement.
"Why are you demanding a timetable in mid-semester?" she retorts….
Disdainfully, she hands me a notepad on which she has scratched basics.

On the road back to my hall of residence, I keep trying to decipher her words
but am accosted each time by a visiting acquaintance, by hunger, by rain.
The notepad tumbles out of my bag again and again, to be mussed by others.
I completely lose track of my boots, my umbrella.

It is only when I am too tired to continue summoning patterns of failure
that I become lucid – lucid enough to remember that intention is all.
Not caring who witnesses, I tell my timetable to stay still until I need it;
and visualise how my umbrella and boots will reappear –
until they do.

A Sequence of Challenges

Cycling uphill, frustrated by trucks
on the incorrect side of a narrowing track,
suddenly I find myself rising high above them,
moving through the air to the conservatoire….
My hands flex to the rhythm of my feet.

The singing lesson is on the ground floor with a friend.
As we practise our scales for the visiting teacher,
I am hoping not to be labelled
"show-off" by the groups gathering behind me.
By the French windows, we stand as a threesome.

Back in my own room, frightened by the volume
of belongings in the main cupboard, I attempt
to un-shelve them…. Scooping up my origami ornaments,
I search around for the lined recycling box:
what I discover is a doll's house wickerwork bowl.

An abrupt gale alarms doors and windows
in distant masonry. Through crannies and vents
it gets to those belongings, whisks them across mosaic tiles.
Its raucousness appals me:
the pull cord is fully disconnected from the light.

Yet after I have done with all these ups and downs,
I allow myself to dream-wonder
whether a gale, a cupboard, groups and trucks
could be seen as a sequence of challenges.
And not a threat.

Monuments

My adoptive parents and I, on arriving in the village,
are yanked right back into the nineteen fifties.
Before me, the Carlton Cinema emerges
with promises of Bambi and Snow White.
In its own cartoons, the Carlton appears to be quirkily drawn:
metamorphosing into an ancient stone monument.

While the sight of a billboard revives my dyslexia,
I can scan the uncertainty in Leighton and Gladys: the denial.
I have quite forgotten the existence of dreams: their signs....
To the right, the main road suddenly swerves:
to the left, the village memorial splits into three.
"It's time to go home," Gladys observes.

     *   *   *

Leighton is concerned with both draughts and regulation:
his wife senses the cold but needs the air....
I fiddle with switches, gas taps and matches.
One of the windows is partially opened
and Gladys reclines beneath it, clothed in a blanket:
she examines the patterns of moisture on glass.

Her dog, Judy, takes me for a walk, then a run.
Someone has warned me: "Avoid Sue!
She's nothing but a fiend dressed in furbelows."
I fail to understand: I know little about Sue.
Sure enough, there she is by the grocer's,
displaying her innocence. I turn away.

Judy runs faster and faster on her corgi legs,
pausing only to yap at the heels of hesitant strollers.
We approach the riverbank, where unforeseen monuments
have so many hexagons and curlicues – such vast facades –
that they petrify….
Detached from her leash, Judy disappears down an alleyway.

As indigo cloud masks the setting sun,
Sue is just behind me; her minions are jeering.
I fly along the alleyway, yelling "Judy!":
find an estuary, a sea – which I feel is much too high
until I realise that the darkening blue is mostly sky.
I plunge into the water …

while Sue, in her role as the infant-woman,
slouches on the beach between Leighton and Gladys –
whose presence astounds me.
Even more than those monuments do.

The Guest

In my own hotel, the bedroom door is ajar.
One of the guests, a tall man in his late thirties,
enters unsolicited.
I am furious, both at myself – for ignoring the key –
and at the man for tousling my morning space.

I bawl at him: "How dare you come in here!"
He scowls, then smiles.
"I need a new bedcover: only the finest will do."
I refuse to consider my one good duvet.
"Get out!" I shout.

After that, he follows me everywhere, his air of triumph
condensed into one of vengeance.
I summon his mother – with whom I have danced in the past –
who lies to me with practised care: "I understand," she murmurs.
My son can do no wrong, is the underlying message.

It is true that in the company of men, he is invariably known for his
charm and wisdom: with me, he is attractive and repulsive in waves.
I find another guest who will be my accomplice:
after stealing away, we are camouflaged in a department store:
we work very hard to rise above the hubbub.

When this brief companion deserts me, I approach the man squarely.
Now in a café, he begins to unbutton my will.
"I am seventy-one," I protest – yet am stilled as if under a spell.
"Who cares about age?" he hisses in my hair
as we lower ourselves to an unswept floor.

The tables are full: we have insufficient room for any play of dominance
and submission. A few heads turn but no one complains:
conditioned by television fantasy and internet fraud, the diners
might well be unshockable. A sudden defiance erupts.
Why should I mind about them? About *him*, for that matter?

When they have gone and we have finished,
he will doubtless leave me alone for good. And he does....
Hours later, I glimpse him outside the hotel – or believe I do –
right under the ivy, snaking around a much younger lover.
The relief, the jealousy: they come in waves.

I Am Swift Purpose

As I drag my baggage along the familiar lane
that leads towards childhood, I sense the beginnings
of a lucid dream: by thought alone,
I can magnetise my cases so that they adhere to each other
very well. I can attach wheels.

It is years since I visited Leighton and Gladys.
They dwell among the clapboard gables
of a hillside estate. On arrival at their home,
I immediately start the unloading, the discarding.

I borrow a waste bin for the smaller items:
the unwieldy ones tumble around it.
The more keenly I focus on symmetry,
the more fretful I become.

I cannot stay here long: it is too enclosed,
too cluttered with Gladys's hairgrips and Leighton's
railway magazines. I walk into the centre of the village
and announce to passers by that not only is this
a dream – but also that they are variations on the dreamer.

For a while, I act the magician, proving my status
by manoeuvring a left finger through my right hand.
"Look! No blood!" I fail to restrain myself.
"See how I levitate!" I rise as far as the rooftops.
"You can do it too," I persist.

There is little response, so I look towards the ironmonger's
and summon a saucepan lid:
stainless steel comes flying into my cupped hope.
I will it to return to its matching pan – till it does.

Fastened at the base of my throat, there is an amethyst brooch
with scalloped edges. More than one person
attempts to remove it: Felix is the last:
he taps on my shoulder before he unclasps it.

I am swift purpose: I glide through the closed doors
of an undertaker's parlour. On its woollen floor
there are twin purple toys: mindful of my brooch,
I lay it to rest between them.

It occurs to me that my role as entertainer is over:
dreams are for self-healing as well as performance.
I can still levitate.

Needing untainted air, I quieten the past
and move westwards. What I require
is nothing less than the sea.

Freed from possession, I learn about patience
as range after range of hills
are unveiled before me.

I keep following the sun – trusting it
to show me the coast.

The Drama Class

Even within the opening scenes of the first act,
I am quick to panic: to forget where my lines begin.
With fingers raised, you have told me the number of the page;
but I am much too fazed to focus, let alone count....
Seconds pass.... No! – I have hold of the wrong script.

Ad-libbing, I burst into a frenzy of excuses
which I twist into the dialogue.
Wendy, Elizabeth and Rosalind refuse to cooperate:
afterwards, I hide from them as fast as I can....
Over and over I have let you down, Frances!

In your role as my producer, you call me to account:
guilty, I both dread and accept whatever I deserve.
"Why?" is the operative word, and you look me
straight in the eye. I repeat what I have claimed on stage:
"I am soon to be homeless," I lie.

Once more, I explain about the women's refuge:
how I have chronic insomnia there;
how unable I am to concentrate.
I feel like a rose without a stem. I apologise –
keeping my voice distinctly low.

Why are you wearing a cashmere sweater and a velvet skirt
if you live in a refuge?" asks Rosalind.
"Perhaps you can tell us where it is," murmurs Elizabeth.
Furious at their talent for discernment,
I reply by walking away –

till you summon me back, describing some childhood game
that you want us to play. I borrow an angular chair –
and watch how the rest of the drama class
forms an ellipse.
You lend me a semi-inflated ball of suede

and prompt me to hurl it right over the students
who are closest….
Not till the fourth attempt can I release it,
or hear its dap between the heels of two men.
Nobody laughs: I cannot see any expression

except yours, Frances, which is not an unfeeling one.
"Try again," you encourage, tapping my hand
with the crooked suede….
If I scold myself often enough, I can do it.
I will do it for you!

Shaking your head, you respond to my unspoken resolve:
"Let go of yourself. And smile while you succeed!"
Rosalind, Wendy and Elizabeth
stand silently, waiting for their turns.
"I can manage *half* a smile," I venture.

A Long Day

After being bussed to a lacklustre academy
on the outskirts of the city,
I am placed where materials are soil,
vegetables and fruit: I arrange dwarf bananas
on a clay hill – until a fellow artist
hints that she can improve on this:
she demolishes my landscape within seconds.

I protest that she has her own task to complete:
how sour my intensity tastes – how it blisters…!

       *   *   *

It is late afternoon: the language teacher
is mopping her corridor. She listens to my fury –
offering one of her youngest cauliflowers.
Perishables will be rotten by the next lesson
but I am comforted by her intentions.

It is almost time to go home. Suddenly, I am handed
my infant son, Gawn. Although he is totally hidden
inside an expensive towel, I can smell that he is damp.
It takes me a while to learn that he is only a doll –
whose caramel head has detached itself from the body
and cannot be found…. It has been a long day!
I cleanse his legs and his trunk in the classroom sink.

Another teacher gives me some sliced melons.
"Put them in the fridge," she instructs me.
I disobey her, preferring to search for my coat:
it has disappeared along with Gawn's doll-head.
"But this is a dream," I remind myself. "And in dreams
I can summon whatever I want." Not only a coat but also
some wellingtons, gloves, scarves, are acquired.

         *   *   *

As I can read neither shop signs nor bus numbers,
I have no idea where I am: I ask a passer-by,
who tells me that I am travelling the wrong way
and need to avoid the docks at all costs.
Being in a dream, I summon a scooter:
grasping its handlebars, I will myself to run uphill,
first on the pavement and then on macadam.

February rain spoils my lapels;
a carrier bag splits its sides:
at the tinkling of my scooter bell, scenery changes
from monuments to lakes to tree-lined fields.
Yet I know that I can see myself home in a trice.
I arrive at the old village, right outside Mumford's
the family grocer's: the door is ajar.

The Concert

I am peevish on board this green, double-decker bus
that is hastening me to a concert: if I were upstairs,
I could see over the hedge and watch the Atlantic….
"Wasn't it you who allotted the seats, Frances?"

When we halt at a roadside café, you say:
"It is your turn, Jennifer, to clean the crockery;
others not chosen for the concert can dry."
You squint at a roster of crumpled names.

The chosen take meals at small, rectangular tables –
panic at the thought of a public performance
deleting any appetite:
their scalloped plates are set aside too soon.

Halfway through my duties, I escape from the kitchen
to search for some sign of a coast.
Felix is in the bus park – happy to avoid me
when I skip across the road to peep through a fence-hole.

Once in the hippodrome, I am angry to find
that only the chosen and their friends are permitted to fill it:
the rest of us lounge in an anteroom, listening
to the warming of sound. A green curtain hangs on the door.

Seventeen minutes into the concert. All of a sudden, a few of us
are pulling at the baize and pushing through the entrance:
we tiptoe up the side aisles
and pause between the platform and the audience …

till Wendy and Rosalind invite us
to dance in a helix. Wendy decides to sing, her light soprano
unfailingly in tune with the voices of the chosen.
At times there is discord, at times resolution. Nobody intervenes.

Focusing on the baroque theme,
I respond above all to the call of the oboe….
You attempt not to observe us, Frances:
you continue to conduct yourself professionally.

When the music is over, the audience applauds
your persistence, and also the mixture of talents.
Your exit is swift. In the lobby, you confront Felix:
the words I catch first are your "travesty" and his "crossover".

Half triumphant, half embarrassed, we linger in the corner.
When Felix lopes towards us, we pretend to be nonchalant:
he extends his arms as far as he can, as if willing us
to blunder and be caught.

"Well done!" he laughs.
"Jennifer, the level of your dancing was particularly high.
And Frances, now you have returned, you can tell us
what is wrong with a sense of humour."

"How could you?" You address me alone.
"Though I admit that you are often forgotten,
nothing disappoints me more than spite. Nothing…."
Felix comes padding to your side: you wince.

"A rebellion leads to a transformation," he states.
"Tomorrow night, I should like to see a repeat –
with no one excluded…."
You are so astonished, Frances – as we all are.

Hair Power

Behind my desk, Rosalind plays with my hair,
which I find hypnotic:
instead of attending to Mrs Gosling's lesson,
I am coiled into euphoria.
Gladys would hate having her scalp touched:
she visits the hairdresser as seldom as possible.

Gradually, I become aware of a firmer hand, a burn:
blades are slicing through my abundant fuzz.
How I jump! Jump!
Cutters clatter on the wood with alarm.
Mrs Gosling looks up. "Jennifer! Elizabeth!"
Her voice yoyos from one register to another.

"She's stolen my hair," I wail, pointing at my classmate –
whose demeanour is inscrutable.
Mrs Gosling is crosser with *me* than with Elizabeth.
"Get on with your note-taking."
She scrapes her domestic science board with a pink chalk.
Scalp flakes litter the backs of my shoulders.

I leap into the apron cupboard, but before I can shut the door
Elizabeth follows. "I've longed to do this for ages," she hisses.
She runs her floured knuckles into the dregs of my frizz:
she recycles my unkindness.
I remain still till she has finished,
then slip from the cupboard to hysterical applause.

"You are dismissed, all of you!" Mrs Gosling bellows.
"Come back when you have calmed down."
As we scurry out, she begins to examine each bowl of ingredients.
In the yard, the girls half envelop me: I would prefer to be ignored.
I remove my apron – which is embroidered with my initials –
and wait by the window for a signal to return. There is none.

       *   *   *

Some time later, on the way home, I am conscious of my namesake
brandishing her own blades. Sharpness arises everywhere –
razors and scissors, of many kinds and colours.
I walk fast but my namesake overtakes me and snips off my fringe.
Fearing for the safety of my forehead, my eyes, I cannot resist.
"We're cutting you down to size," Rosalind quips.

Both at home and at school, I become an embarrassment.
"What a mess!" Gladys exclaims – remembering how, when I was five,
I chopped at my curls: remembering how she cried.
Mrs Gosling, while emerging from her larder, concludes:
"You must work it out among yourselves. You are old enough."
We are twelve.

The best way to deal with such hostility
is to outface it, I feel: to outstare every jot of it.
But the loss of my hair has weakened any gazing-power:
has tired me so much that I can only apologise
for previous unkindness –
and for a dozen other wrongs that I have never inflicted.

Inappropriately, perhaps, I am reminded of Samson and Delilah –
even of the shorn inhabitants of Bergen-Belsen....
Well, I do know my Torah –
and they say that my hair is typical for an Ashkenazi Jew.

The Crash

I am travelling to England with my son, Gawn:
the aircraft sounds unstable – but as usual I relax
into a near-sleep state
in which time no longer exists.

Lightning happens: it pitches me into a whiteout of fear.
Turbulence forces us to fasten our seatbelts,
then bruisingly grounds us.
According to the pilot, we remain within the State of New York.

His plane taxies; almost collides with a convoy of trucks: I faint.

     *   *   *

I recover at my parents': in their East of England kitchen,
Leighton is cooking a light meal.
Looking out of the French window, I catch the aircraft
attempting acrobatics to the west of the garden.
I am glad to be out of it.

After the inevitable crash, I can sense only guilt
at my abandonment of Gawn: I am drawn
to that field where the craft is in fragments.
Not a sign of any fire.

In due course, dazed passengers totter into view:
when Gawn appears, I yell his name again and again
but he fails to listen. It occurs to me that Leighton and I
have had no conversation today whatsoever.
Did he realise that I was there?

        *   *   *

A nurse explains that I need to be examined:
fears are now impacted as tubes and swabs
are inserted and applied for an hour or so.
"What can you remember?" a doctor enquires.
I describe my awakening in the Fens: the flailing plane.

"You're still in the USA," she insists.
"You may go home soon – tomorrow, perhaps."
Being half American, I am glad to be detained
yet feel confused. "How is my son?" I ask.
"Oh, he's a great little kid. The odd swelling, that's all."

        *   *   *

When the moment comes to locate my seat on the Wednesday plane,
I watch how a dog – a German Shepherd – poises nearby:
a label on its collar reveals the name, which I make myself
pronounce twice – with a smile; with a smile.

As we fly towards the sun, fears imperceptibly thaw….
Fritz – therapy dog that he is – will doze with his head in my lap
till I am warmed enough to admit more clarity.

Make Believe

A mature, conceptual artist
drops from a rooftop:
he lands with a bounce
and I see that he is wearing
a thick fluffy jumpsuit.

One of his students rises
towards an abundance of blues:
when he descends, I notice
that a green trampoline
has been camouflaged by grass.

     *   *   *

I need to prepare for the reading aloud
of my spring term's poems;
so why have I skipped to my home
rather than dining at school?

Felix has insisted on driving me back:
I wait by the door – soothed by the texture
of lozenges and glossy print….
His arrival fails to be early enough.

"The Queen will be there," I remonstrate.
"I wanted to give her a copy of my book:
she has so many connections!"

"I have no time at all for the Monarchy,"
Felix declares. "Nor for the Tooth Fairy –
nor for Santa Claus, as a matter of fact."

I rattle my childhood moneybox.
"The Tooth Fairy is the only one
who suggests that I save," I argue.
"The best Father Christmas I know
is my cousin: he dances in the snow."

   *   *   *

I turn to my suitcase:
it loiters in the alleyway.
"Be off with you!" I command.
My back aches and I lack wheels.

The leathery trunk skids along the lane,
begins to ascend towards what is now
an accumulation of grays.

It travels so warily above me
that I doubt its ability to go further:
it falls to the ground, right at my feet….

Faking belief till it becomes firm,
I send the case on its mission once more.
Perhaps I could direct it to the Queen –
or the Tooth Fairy; or Santa Claus.

The Besom

I lean forward, sweeping each classroom with a fervour
that I usually reserve for paving stones.
It is late July: both pupils and staff have left me far behind –
except for Natalie, the dance teacher.
From her bench by the entrance, she beckons with a slim hand.

"I have good news," she begins.
"If you go to the village ironmonger's,
they will give you a pass for The Hall On The Hill.
I'm organising a festival there and I'd like you to be part of it."

When we have taken our leave of her, my besom and I,
we immediately fly across the games pitch, the lanes –
finally touching down at Wally Long's.
It is after hours: the letterbox clenches my pass….
"Natalie told me to expect you," yells Wally.

      *   *   *

While following signs for The Hall On The Hill,
I observe that Veronica's lodge has an open door:
a curve of women advances towards it with valuable gifts.
Hurt that I am uninvited, I decide to join in.

No one seems to notice my arrival –
even when I sit down at the dining table.

Veronica is a temptress of a cook:
forgetting that Gladys provides my meals
and ignoring the audition,
I am conscious of more than one level of hunger.

The hostess approaches with her trolley of hors d'oeuvres.
On seeing me, she gasps. "Jennifer! What are *you* doing here?"
Up goes her chin. Her guests grow silent.

"You have an open door," I remind her.
"Also, you have often protested that I am too thin…."
Veronica shakes her head. The women beside me exhibit their backs:
I anticipate textures, aromas and flavours.

        *   *   *

Mindful of Natalie, I excuse myself, pick up the besom
and continue on my journey to The Hall On The Hill.

An audition is no longer an option:
I sweep, sweep the community plot till I burn.

        *   *   *

Curious to know what has happened at Veronica's,
I return to her lilac house.
The door remains ajar. I enter. The table is bare, so I call out,
"Is anyone there?"

Longing for drama, I imagine until it is real
that a sinister atmosphere permeates the place.
Clasping my besom, "Is anyone there?" I repeat, repeat….
The larynx fails.

As soon as I am outside again,
I plant my possession in the front garden
and do an elaborate dance on the crazy paving.
At once, faces are in windows –
some full of wonder, others derisive.

I increase the intensity of my performance.
Someone shouts. "What *are* you – a witch?"
"Of course!" I croak. "If you watch very carefully,
you'll see me on my broomstick!"

Natalie's Peugeot appears by the gates: I feel ashamed.
"Jennifer, it's time you came home," she advises.
"Gladys has been looking for that besom. Everywhere."

Half laughing, half sobbing, I pull my reliable tool from the soil
and carry it safely to her car.

Finding My Bearings

I am fully awake in my dream – in an oriental quarter
whose neon bears names that I fail to translate:
above the café bars, each character jumps at my dyslexia.

Sometimes, signs come in my own language.
"Where *am* I?" I say to the woman passing by.
"Why, The Honch," she replies – offering nothing more.

Is this the entertainment of an island?
It is hardly any stranger than being in the otherlife:
many of the tourists have American accents.

       *   *   *

I move towards mountains, float over their craters –
choosing to drop like a leaf from a canopy
into the matt gray valleys.

To the west, the volcanic ash makes way for the pasture:
there is moisture on my wrist: I inhale the scent
till my brow becomes heavy.

The next moment, I find myself at the home of the woman
who spoke so briefly.
Almost apologetically, she lends me a couch.

       *   *   *

Rested, I believe that I am now within the otherlife;
but the view through the window is of lanterns and ponds
that I have never known.

To prove that I am dreaming, I begin
by pressing my thumbs against a mahogany panel:
it yields like a sponge.

In the otherlife, I once had appointments, dependants:
something has kept me away. Did I die there…?
It is only then that the dream gradually leaves….

        *   *   *

Determination cuts in: searching online
for even one picture to match where I have been,
I come to The Honch, Yokosuka, Japan.

Maeve

Ousted by my landlady, I receive no direction: my adoptive parents are
reluctant to comment. When I disappoint them, I am "Jennifer dear":
when I please, Leighton calls me Piecrust. In his garden, he addresses
the lawn: "Mummy believes you must fend for yourself – Jennifer dear."

There is a hostel for the homeless in the bowels of this town
that I try to ignore. But the twilight and my hunger
drive me into its doorway, its rectangular hall
where women and men – mostly women – pause below the windows.

The warden listens: she tuts at my refined clothes, my neat pronunciation.
An obese man – a previous resident? – offers me a floor in his
neighbouring house…. "I am not so easily taken in," I whisper –
backing away from his whisky lips.

"You may stay here for six nights," I am told. A rubbery finger points
to the staircase: beds are in the basement. I examine the steps, see them
become a deformed spiral from the oblong hall to the crypt.
I refuse to put one toe on them.

It is safer to slip outside, creep down the hill and enter the basement
through a back door. There is one washbasin for ten women and two men;
one toilet. Tomorrow, I will search for somewhere bright: tonight,
I am so tired that, as soon as I am prone, I fall asleep.

The mattress begins to travel: it carries me into the ocean….
In the morning, I remember my appointment with a surgeon.
"I am fully aware of your teeth," snaps the warden. Before I can reply,
she accompanies me to the hospital, where I am anaesthetised.

The procedure is over before it has begun – or so it seems. My tongue is
numb. "You may drink through a straw." My question is answered
just as I think of it. I return to the hostel with Maeve –
who is prematurely white: who is everyone's mother; twin sister; lover:

who comes to my bed at the end of the night to comfort my mouth.
It hurts me to admit that, despite the peeling damp, the threadbare cold
and brusque warden, I am starting to like this place:
it has an air of acceptance.

And then I know…. I wake the entire hostel with a new voice:
"We are linked to each other by a dream. Watch!" I insert my finger
into a worktop: I extract it, and wait for the hole to disappear.
I make for the ceiling and dance in the air. "Join me, if you wish."

Even though most of them are stunned, no one grows hostile.
After my descent, it is Maeve who takes me by the hand:
"What role do *I* play?" Her tone is as gentle as Leighton's.
"The wise woman," I say…. Smiling, she leads me to my breakfast.

Hoping for Venus

With a taupe cylinder in the hand,
and toes just inches above the oily ground,
I begin my long ascent – drawn to the promise
of a *Great Surprise on Attaining the Summit.*

Batteries for climbs are so quick to run down!
Frequently, I halt: I select those gates
where a tool may engage with a keyhole;
become invigorated.

How common it is for silver to seem off colour!
At the seventh gate, it triggers a fund of water
that cannot cease till it alerts. The subsequent furore
is a lean tenant parading his lungpower.

All of a sudden, I turn left: I drift along the street
to an indigo garage. The mechanic greets me
as though I were his daughter: he listens: he grins
at my delinquent batteries

and conjures up another set, in a stainless-steel case.
"This will take you straight to the top," he declares,
"without stopping." He lays its cool on my curious palm
and escorts me to the highway –

where the traffic spills its oils, and the queue before the red sign
lengthens by the second. Now, I can move beyond them.
The bespoke cylinder increases my speed
till I come to a tunnel that is lined with luminous moss.

It leads to a building whose glazed eyes overlook the valley,
and whose forehead is engraved with the words: *Welcome
to the Great Treat. Enjoy….* It is not as I imagined
but I enter the foyer and follow the arrows

to a television lounge. In front of its
mumbling screens, the people are being assembled….
In a while – faced as I am with the backs of their heads –
I remember the steel: how it makes me rise.

But what is there to view? A recorded royal wedding
or Olympic triumph, no doubt. Can anyone tell me
what more to expect? Do I *need* to be told…?
I would like to be alone in the dusk – hoping for Venus.

All or Nothing

Following the lightness and darkness of our dancing,
Natalie prepares us for the making of a collage
with her lawn's feathered bones; its petals and thorns….
The title is *Contrast: a Reflection of Ourselves.*

She forbids us to behead flowers or strip saplings.
My demon, taking the shape of a foetus, understands little
but ensures that I feel his neediness, as he kicks
from the womb in my mind. "Do nothing," he commands.

And I obey him – for an hour or two –
while the other dancers run onto the lawn
and gather whatever their exuberance can bear….
In a wide circle around Natalie, they place

rough below smooth, stinging behind soothing,
angular opposite curved.
Defying both teacher and demon, I begin by
wrenching the heads off red and white roses,

by stealing a pebble from the neighbouring beach –
an oval that comes with a history of grays.
I carry it all on the plate with the indigo rim.
Indoors is so full that I crouch on the floorboards.

Lateness fails to be observed: my demon tells me
to interrupt quickly: I shout before I can wilt.
"Look at my colours: the blood and the bloodless,
the somethings and nothings that we call gray!"

No one notices: I linger in the queue for the kitchen
where meals are rewards for skills and cooperation.
Not hungry, I return to the living room,
whose artwork becomes a mandala. Mine is not there –

only the plate with its dark perimeter: I sniff: no fragrance.
Elizabeth spots my disappointment: she has seen how I
plucked my heads; has disapproved; and is bewildered.
When lunchtime has ended, Natalie upbraids me.

She points to the vacant plate. "What do you mean by this?" she asks.
"Nothing," I reply. "There is no contrast. I am nothing…."
My demon is pleased, but I half sense that I am lying.
"A void within a crowd," Elizabeth says. "Perhaps we need one."

From Sluggard to Hummingbird

Leon turns left into The Triangle as though he were
on call, then makes for the drive of Number Eleven.
The home is not alarmed: brandishing his key,
he proceeds to unlock its pink door.

It is a while since we lived here: in the lounge, I remark
on the nuanced improvements, the removal of clutter.
But in the dining room, the first detail I notice
is a minuscule slug, moistening itself on the hearthrug.

Gastropods without shells have an uncertain reputation:
I lift it to safety, laying it down beside a cactus….
What an odd mollusc it is – toughening the skin,
changing the tone from orange-brown to bright green!

   *   *   *

It is now an iguana and can run quite fast.
Leon distrusts it: hurrying into the garden
he thrusts it as high as he can.

After it has morphed into a hummingbird,
it performs a figure of eight for the sun.

Anticipating loss, I am relieved
when it dives into the grass –
and returns to being a sluggard.

* * *

Exploring the house, we remain so absorbed
that we scarcely take in the arrival of the owners,
Grant and Elaine; they are accompanied by a young boy....
As Leon repairs to the bathroom, I attempt to explain.

It is strange that neither of these parents recognises me.
"I am Gossamer Webbe," I lie. Through the window, I glimpse
the *For Sale* sign. "The estate agent gave me a key ..."
"She shouldn't have," Grant interrupts.

"Are you thinking of buying?" Elaine ignores him.
"Gossamer's a funny name," the boy butts in.
Is it real or pretend?" An eyelid twitches.
"Oh, pretend, of course," I double-bluff.

Grant questions Leon through the bathroom casement.
"No, I am not Mr Webbe, and *Jennifer* is my wife's name"
is the one response I can catch.

I kneel in front of the boy and suggest
that we go into the garden to discover something special.
"Mummy can come too, "I reassure him.

Elaine frowns and follows us, the child skipping ahead.
"I'm Christopher!" he yells.

    *   *   *

All of us are on the lawn, observing how slug
switches into iguana, then hummingbird.
Christopher claps. "More, more!" he roars.
The creature obliges until it collapses.

Arrested at the lizard stage, it sleeps by the cactus.
Elaine begins to giggle: Leon and Grant
have smiles in their eyes.
Christopher fingers the tail, the scales.

Promising that we will never again trespass,
I witness the retained key being handed over.
"If I were you," Leon advises, "I'd change the lock."

Christopher minds the iguana.

Polarities

I climb to the top floor – to the studio-home of an Old Master:
its authentic grime is encouraged by the university –
or so I am told.

Stig appears: claims that *he* is the painter:
he is neither a ghost nor a master.

Facing north, he exhibits primary tints in order to
rebel against the dust.

           *   *   *

Entering into a genderless dance, I soon discover myself
in the role of Natalie, the tutor.

This hall doubles as a chapel.
Not dissuaded by the saintly flyer on the cupboard,
I lift red petals from the centrepiece, and flaunt them in my hair.

Natalie's eyes narrow. "What *is* it with you?" she asks.
"Energy likes to be shared," I reply. Her students glare.

Moments later, they are copying whatever I do.
In the end, when I rest on the wood-sprung floor,
Natalie relents, and lies down among them.

           *   *   *

Fasting is another kind of resting: the refectory is closed.
Rescuing a tray from the corridor outside it …
is my duplicate…! Shock wrong-foots me: we nearly collide.

Enter my namesake. She brings me the bitterest of fruit.
"Eat this," she orders. I obey – which is not the expected response.

"How simple it is to look through you!" She stands to attention.
"You dominate with tantrums – and show off your cowardice.
"You think you have clarity – yet practise distortion."

"Like Stig, I am drawn to polarities," I answer:
"to the paradox and flux that are growing between them."

Hot Moon

On the Californian coast, Gladys, Leighton and I
have slept in a workshop; and woken in our dreams.
Judy the corgi excites the lawn before midsummer sun
can burn her into submission.

In the Hexagon Room, twelve of us are invited
to be mindful of our hearts: to ask for what we desire most.

"Inspiration!" I am always the first to follow a pause....
A voice bounces into my left ear. "Stop moving your hips!"

Fazed by the abruptness of his command, I cry out:
"Can't inspiration be born from a sway –
as well as from a tableau?" This hypocrite beside me
has a narrow hand that fidgets on my shoulder.

Pulling away, I begin to listen to an eight-part chorale
whose texture both grounds and arouses.

      *   *   *

In the interlude, I search in vain for Leighton and Gladys –
and make my enquiries at the Lost and Found.

Judy is missing also. I enter the animal guesthouse
to replenish the bowl and let in the breeze.

The news is unusually slow. A corgi has been seen
jollying up its folks on the Pacific shoreline.

Afterwards, looking into the sky, I acknowledge
how confident the Hot Moon becomes
in its cloudlessness.

Anaemia

I confine my poems to a listed building –
scribble them in brick-powder on the top storey.
The mezzanine floor remains openly drowsy, its book-tower
propping up the emporium's knitwear.

When I leave through an archway,
I encounter a saleswoman at her desk –
who seems oblivious of any fallen masonry,
any rickety appliance: I try hard to warn her.
Her fingertips are bloodless.

        *   *   *

In the basement, my namesake has rescued
a manikin that is a young brother:
on the wagon home, we wait with him at the front....
I am unprepared for what happens.

The Leech family gapes at us from their side seats
as the infant is lowered onto a bench and sedated:
one of his eyes is almost closed; he feels no pain
as his sister begins to delve into the soft head –
to scoop out dollops of jelly.

"Are you playing at being a surgeon or an artist?" I hiss.
Her answer is terse: "Can't I be both…?"
At least, there is no blood.

           *   *   *

At the end of the journey, the Leeches follow us
as far as our driveway: I can smell their curiosity.
Felix, the owner, informs us that we are moving house:
he has half completed touching up the staircase;
has gullible viewers queuing in the back yard.

"This town will soon be a beggars' mausoleum," he predicts,
nodding in the direction of
supermarkets without tills, roofs without tiles.

I object: "How I will miss the sea!"
"But the sea is already encroaching," he reminds me.

When the Leech family withdraws, I can feel my anxiety plummet.
Now, I remember: over ninety percent of my plasma is water:
my blood, weak though it is, cries out to the Atlantic….
Carrying the manikin, I dance into the high tide.
Unafraid.

Cartoon

Home from hospital with a new hip –
with Arnica Montana on my bruises and swellings –
I sleep fitfully….

It is noon in the village: I recognise the place
by its various gables and chimneys,
by the pinks of its paving stones.

The hurdy-gurdy resounds before I observe it:
gliding into view is a childhood float
complete with its cartoon cast.

A plastic rabbit with an oval face
and a pompous voice
climbs high above the rest.

I feel so uneasy about this buck
that I cannot speak. Half awake by now,
I register the pain in my bones:

how it throbs in time to the music.
At regular intervals, the buck's head sinks
into the huge, blueing dewlap –

only to emerge with a sickening judder….
I try to wake fully but am led towards a dwarf cottage
where the cartoon menagerie waits for its feast.

I listen to the woman with the ebony hair
that sticks out from her temples.
She resembles one of those monochrome gables –

is entirely unaware that I will occupy her psyche....
The music stops: the rabbit responds with a fattened yawn.
My pain gone, I anticipate nothing but food.

A straw man limps past.
I glance out of the lattice window
in time to see the raven poised on a gatepost.

A clock strikes. I am brought back to the otherlife,
knowing that my keywords – *little*, and *slow* –
are ones that I like.

Chagrin

Back at university with Amy – specialist in limpets –
we welcome our friends on a lawn that has no seat.
Mornings are moist: Amy invites me to her blanket, her lap.

Occasionally, I doze …
am startled to see her double in the distance.
Yet I know that she has never been twinned.

Turning round, I find that I am leaning against
a Native Canadian, who grunts and scowls:
perhaps she is used to ousting her descendant!

Dawdling towards the tutorial halls
and approaching the steepest of hills, I realise
that I am dreaming and can rise with ease.

On arrival at my cliff-top destination, I am introduced
to the newly appointed, salmon-haired professor.
The Native Canadian has gone: Amy comes in with a whisper,

takes me aside. "About the professor: they are proud
to be bi-gender; are prepared to be incisive and blunt
in a single go. In secret, they expect to be confronted."

I observe them: they plump for a premature lunch.
It includes onions, to which I am allergic:
in the pocket of my jacket, I have six emergency biscuits.

Needing the toilets,
I leave the tutorial hall to look for the relevant sign.
What I discover is more like a study than a cloakroom –

with devotees bent on perfecting their essays.
On each desk, there is a piss-pot shaped like a vase.
As there is an absence of odour

I presume that none has been touched.
A maroon throne has been fixed to the floor
for those who are brave enough to defecate.

I search in vain for a lid.
"Where is the aperture?" I ask the one scholar
who has raised his head.

How embarrassed he is!
The chair, unlike the distressed desks,
is so thoroughly buffed that it cannot be used.

Amy is in the corridor, her arms extending towards me.
"Why not try the otherlife for a while…?"
So I do.

1 Woller Gardens

Not until our last dance do we become conscious
of the trio that observes us. Unnerved, we creep down
to a sunken lawn – to the solace of a limestone swan;
of a table frequented by starlings and sparrows.

We do not hear the footsteps on the clover: we listen to the birds,
their sudden murmuration. To my left, one of the observers
arrives with a strident cry: my companions are silent.
He addresses me by name.

"Give me that shoulder bag." I am the only dancer
who possesses one with nine pockets. Handing it over,
I am angrily bemused. This thug is obese and as pink as a baby,
has eyes that could turn from silver to navy at the flick of a knife.

Neither money nor identity intrigues him. "Look at this!"
Extracting my mobile phone, he beckons to his two colleagues.
"How have you come by this number?" he asks me.
His eyes begin to darken: I fix mine on his many chins.

He howls: then reels off the eleven digits.
"How do you know this person?" he yells. I swallow.
I glance at the sculpture of the Dying Swan – at a solo sparrow.
"I know neither the number nor its owner…."

Foreign words riddle the air; his underlings obey him
by grasping my elbows: my companions disappear.
Those hitman's eyes become black slits: sun sets
in a duvet of coral and gold. October's wind is cold.

As a mini-truncheon pushes against my eyeball
I scream: "No! I am innocent! Innocent…!"
I scream till I am gagged and half blinded.

        *   *   *

Coming to, I sense how the oblong room
pulses with fury; how threats, both ancient and recent,
dart along the skirting board. Although I have sight,
there is little relief: I visualise a Celtic cross.

When I wake for the second time, the room becomes a square –
its window exposing a landscape bare of trees.
It is a while before I test my tongue, or finger the doorknob.
I find I am alone, without mirrors – and am glad of such absence.

The Promise

The November tides have toyed for hours
with Gawn, Veronica and me:
it is Gawn who decides to turn away, to stay alone.

No sooner have Veronica and I set foot in my house
than a telephone rings. The police:
they have found my son on the ground, unconscious –

have assumed that his malaise comes from an alcoholic binge.
Veronica intervenes. "Does his breath smell of almonds?"
I think of cyanide within its ridged bottle.

When we are told that Gawn has been taken to hospital –
the nineteen thirties one, with its imitation Dutch gables –
we drive there immediately, uncertain which entrance to approach.

The moment we have walked through the doors on the left
we are questioned, and placed in an apprehensive queue.
Eventually, an orderly admits us to her ward.

Beds jut out from opposing walls: Gawn is in the corner.
It is difficult to judge how much of him is bruised or broken.
The nurse begins to feed him pink paste from a dessertspoon –

a mixture that snakes out of his mouth only minutes afterwards.
She scrapes the rejected medicine from his blanket
with a serrated knife – then points the steel at me.

"Aren't you his mother? *You* can deal with this."
I spring forward, then recoil when she deliberately flicks
regurgitated pink at my cheek, my violet coat.

I report her to the ward manager – who is unapologetic.
"Some of my nurses are like that: they are so overworked!"

I practise understanding.

The very next morning, Gawn is wheeled to the left –
towards the exit. Taking hold of his feet, I hear myself saying:

"I love you…. You *will* recover."

Bessie

"Do you like it when there are changes?" I ask Bessie.
"I do!" she laughs: we are on the coach that speeds from the city
to those flatter roads and wider skies of Lincolnshire.

When we approach an octagonal mansion,
neither of us can read its name, because of our dyslexia.
The driver agrees to leave us there.

Our tickets are available at the white gate:
we wait in a side room the shape of an almond.
The child looks at a painting of stars.

Someone is offering tumblers of juice.
"Mummy says I mustn't talk to strangers." Bessie frowns.
Despite this, I sip the liquid – which has a peculiar flavour.

A few minutes later, my limbs begin to feel heavy.
A group of us is ushered into the ground floor parlour,
which is filled with Victoriana.

Upstairs, I pause until the guide moves on:
pulling off my sandals, I climb into a four-poster bed.
Bessie sits quietly on the window seat, keeping watch….

After some time, I emerge from the quilt
to follow her down to the entrance hall.
I tell her to pick whatever she likes from its gift corner.

She selects a photograph of hot springs.
"I noticed them from the bedroom window," she explains.
I think of New Zealand; Italy; Japan …

"Anything can happen in Wonderland," Bessie claims –
and I realise for the first time
how tall she has grown since we arrived.

       *   *   *

"Who's going to collect us? Nana?" she enquires….
I have failed to register that no bus passes by –
that trains have been absent for more than fifty years.

I deal with my panic by hoisting her onto my shoulder –
she is a young child again. I remember my mobile
but drowsiness prevents me from using it.

Questions belong in the annexe – which is about to close:
I mention our dyslexia, our need for a taxi.
The clerk is in his overcoat. "Cabs are unobtainable," he barks.

       *   *   *

Once Bessie is tall enough, I point to the vintage car outside
with its unlocked doors, its key in the ignition.
"Have you passed your test?" I hint…. Her gaze is unfocused.

Amy is in touch with our coach driver: she beckons from her Skoda
and invites us to join her. Bessie makes for the back.
"She's been waxing and waning for hours," I yawn.

The grandmother glances at the girl in the mirror.
"Hi, little moon," she whispers. "Have you seen the hot springs?"
Bessie smiles. "Yes, Nana! I shone right through them."

A Fragile Blue

After the rehearsal, Felix and I come home to Gladys –
whose foggy heart responds to a hot kitchen;
whose third eye, a toy one, is in the wrong position –
lower than the others, on the left side of her face.

Constantly, she maintains that it never sees:
whenever she wants, she allows herself
to pluck it out from under its black brow.
Her main brows are a faint gray.

She demonstrates: I gaze into a dark socket –
look at its disconnected jelly.
"May I hold it?" I ask. Cautiously, she hands it over.
"I'm going to the show," she tells me.

Felix will drive her to the school hall
to hear me reading my poem based on a vision.
It will finish itself while I float up the hill
to the downs and the playing fields.

Felix insists on inspecting the eye:
"It belongs to me," he claims – much to my surprise.
"It has powers that Gladys cannot dream of."
The only dream of hers was to have a son.

As soon as they have gone –
Gladys as wardrobe mistress, Felix as director –
I recite part of an earlier poem to the oblong mirror:
"Out of its element, nothing can flourish …"

What was once an eye has changed
into a semi-opaque tadpole –
which I cradle within a cupped palm.
The amphibian swells: I tip it into a bowl of water.

   *   *   *

As I drift uphill above twilight puddles,
it jumps out and disintegrates.
I am about to ignore what has happened
when it begins to repair itself

and allows me to lift it up….
The second time it leaps out of the water
I let it disappear, knowing that I will be late
for the performance if I stop to search.

I arrive at the school to find Felix in the foyer.
"*You've* taken your time!" he scolds.
In the rooms below, Gladys attends
to her costumes…. All of her eyes are a fragile blue.

On the Road to Hope Cove

At the end of March, I journey home
with familiar scholars; pyramids of luggage.
It is cramped and unsanitary: instead of a closet
there are chamber pots – scattered, as if to trip us up.

When our driver becomes too unwell to continue,
we are stranded between hedgerows. On my left is O'Brien:
the eccentric playmate; the knighted professor –
whose greengrocer parent compares him to an exotic fruit.

On my right, Megan remains focused:
ever since withdrawing from the corps de ballet
with an injured spine, she has worked with the remnants
of her bitterness, the very marrow of them.

Behind me, a bed supports my adoptive father –
or is it my grown son? Both suffer from bouts of amnesia.
When a student brings him a tincture of rosemary
and ginkgo biloba, he refuses to be tempted.

Time to connect with our next of kin: I consult my mobile.
A few of my companions begin to complain.
"Why don't we summon a taxi or two?" Megan suggests.
O'Brien takes charge. "We have enough resources," he confirms.

The whole fleet arrives in its navy blue paint: I am strangely relieved
that our previous driver has vanished – stolen our luggage.
I choose a front seat for my parent-cum-child: simultaneously,
he opens the door to his memory; his daydreams.

Facade

The artist-in-residence looks on her employer
as an elderly child.

Her security task is to hand out forms
for the signing of names:
clearly, without my lenses, I cannot find
the correct space.

Agitated by the abrupt queue,
the girl abandons it:
she tucks a free admittance card
into my slippery pocket.

All around me hang paintings
in dominant corals and yellows –
their focused lights too bright
for me to concentrate.

   *   *   *

The president appears in the doorway,
his half-smile inviting us to follow him.

How easy it is to pretend that I like him –
to stand on the right side!
How quickly he seems to be convinced!
Even the dogs on his left
are more intelligent than that.

When lies become tiresome,
I make my way through a stuccoed wall
to the backyard –
where one of those muscular curs
rushes at me, snarling.

I have learned how to win ferocity over
with tamed words –
to ensure that it does no more
than lather my palms with a slack tongue.

I am quite unaware of trespassing
on a peculiar zone –
until the president himself
reluctantly accosts me.

      *   *   *

Turning away from a fine facade,
I enquire about homeward flights.

A guard detains me with questions….
"Why not look behind you?" he mocks.

With my lenses, I can see that the west garden
accommodates nothing but a toy plane.

Acting Out

"You will never amount to anything," my teacher pronounced
when I strove for attention by doing nothing.

After my piano lesson, I balanced on a terracotta wedge
by the front porch. Gladys told the tutor, "She's no credit to me."

Could she have been joking – or was it a sign of resignation?
At the age of nine, how could I tell?

       *   *   *

Now, I am a young man in my imagination –
with straight, blond hair; with a longing to change my agenda.

In my room there is a dead fish, so thickly embalmed
in its waterless tank that it lacks the relevant malodour.

In my hand, there is a bottle containing an unknown chemical:
once released, it hurls you into a well of sleep.

       *   *   *

I practise in a concert hall – a deconsecrated chapel on the hill
that fills itself with what Gladys calls "your elders and betters".

Nobody suspects me, or remains awake when spraying is over.
Certainly, I am no credit to anyone: I strive no more for attention

but busy myself with covering the bottle – with acknowledging
that seafood, however well embalmed, remains frail.

On Platform 9, a film is continuously projected
onto a blank wall – until it is broken by floater-like dots….

In the chapel on the hill, a cellist has woken up confused, furious.
In denial as I ride home, I focus my thoughts on the glazed tank.

     *   *   *

I have carried my creel to a languid bay – have waited for the waves
to reappear with unparalleled force…. I return their former inhabitant.

My bottle is empty: no harm has been done. My doctor approaches
and asks how I feel. "Good," I lie. "I am just very tired…."

OCTET

Shanklin Rain

All this July day, soft rain has soaked
my orange American cotton:
I have walked through a chine
that is like a subtropical biome.

Under the platform's roof,
the station clock makes dripping sounds.
A small woman talks to herself on a painted bench
to assuage the loneliness –
her voice, like that of a radio broadcaster,
switched on and off … and on …
Behind us, a waiting room is locked.

Outside, mist nets the east cliff;
while diesel and steam, with their different
rhythms and gauges,
take visitors, commuters, backwards and forwards
like a pendulum, a tide.

On the Other Side

On the other side of the track,
you pass through a second kissing gate.

Canopied by a beech, you negotiate the rising of steps –
the unevenness of five.

A six o'clock breeze punctuates your heat:
the moon turns half diaphanous.

On the other side,
old wildness comes in purples and golds; soft whites.

The crickets are in their grasses:
branches embrace, safe within their archways.

A white bird glides over the water, moving west:
a black crab hastens towards an estuarial stone.

In your own good time, you will accompany this river, Isca,
as it falls into the sea.

"Not now," you say aloud.

Later on, turning round in a homeward field – turning west –
you notice those roses, those vermilion heads above the hedgerow.

From the other side of the railway track, they are calling you back....
You are warned.

"Not now," you repeat. "Not now."

Camaraderie in the Margins

I rest in my sleevelessness,
watching the sea mist silver the sun:

two canoeists make for what is left of its reflection.

Young men sit in their fearlessness,
bragging about exam grades –

till one of them, desperate for balance,
indicates an insect on his skateboard.

"Come and see the ladybug," he pleads….

Camaraderie in the margins:
I have noticed it before,
on the borders of lochs and forests –

even in dystopian twitchels and ginnels.

The Host of the Holly

To a host of sparrows, home is the holly bush….
By the end of December, between storms,
the twilight sound of it tastes like raisins, orange rind.

The following morning, each bird
claims its place on the neighbouring rooftop –
sensing the river, the Exe, which has risen with the downpour.

The plumpness that comes is an East Devon herring gull:
the purpose is to bully,
to usurp the community perch.

But the host is used to this:
its rapid wings carry it to and fro between ridge and ridge –
till the game becomes dull.

Whenever a bird flies *solo* from its line –
perhaps to alight on the cowl or the aerial –
familiar sidesteps close the gap.

In spite of the heft of her tartan trolley, her birdcage umbrella,
the woman treads quietly on the twilight pavement:
she approaches the feathery belly of the holly – its prickly guards.

An only child, she is drawn towards extended families:
she choreographs for community dancers:
her poems are appreciated most when read aloud.

Tempest

This titan of a gale
makes pendulums out of shop signs.

The road's bollards are disabled.

Lifted over the licked stone
by promenade gusts,
flotsam is a kiosk – candyfloss, lollipops!

Beneath where it used to stand,
a bomb, unexploded for seventy years,
silences at once those tidal spectators.

Electric flexes go wild in the heightened water:
sparks are launched into quarrelsome sky.

In response to this crescendo of extremes,
the town is alight with euphoria, with terror –
not knowing one from the other.

As the sea lays claim to the plains it once covered,
the people become eccentric; chaotic:
are seduced by the drama of it all.

After the panic, there follows the need
to control, to capture –

if only in pictures on the screens of their phones.

Crouch

Just before the black van parks in the square,
panic begins with herring gulls piercing the sky:
most of them no longer keep their nests
close to the sea.

The Harris Hawk comes complete with his falconer's glove,
with jesses attached to his brilliant feet:
the man has a dream about freedom from scavengers.

In intelligent bursts, the bird flies hither and thither
at the word of his master, the command to scare:
herring gulls, pigeons, are not to be devoured….
Prized for his performance, he dines on steaks.

"Crouch," cries the falconer. "Crouch…."
All of his hawks have footballers' names.
Children are amused: they are queuing like fans:
they long to touch feathers, the leather of the glove.

From time to time, this particular raptor delays his return:
he alights on an outdoor table, waiting to be photographed,
or makes for the indoor market, the souvenir stand.

Banished from the square,
from its human detritus,
the herring gulls move to the cliffs.

Not Knowing

"Life is no longer a feast of
distractions from death:

all I can sense are those
twin grizzly roads: at no point do they meet.

You are here, my friend, not only for tea and raspberries
but also to make enquiries, to listen."

"Tell me what grows within your gray," you say.

"A pink rose." I surprise myself.
"But I still don't wish to live," I remind you.

"I don't wish to live *like this*," you respond.

It's the not knowing I can't cope with….
"When I have done with both bone and brain," I continue,
"will consciousness remain…?
What if it won't? What will have been its point?"

"Does there have to be a point?" you challenge.

"This vision of parallel roads," I persist –
"roads without even one byway between them –
is anathema to me.

Death has become a distraction from living –
from interconnection."

"Though not for the rose," you observe.

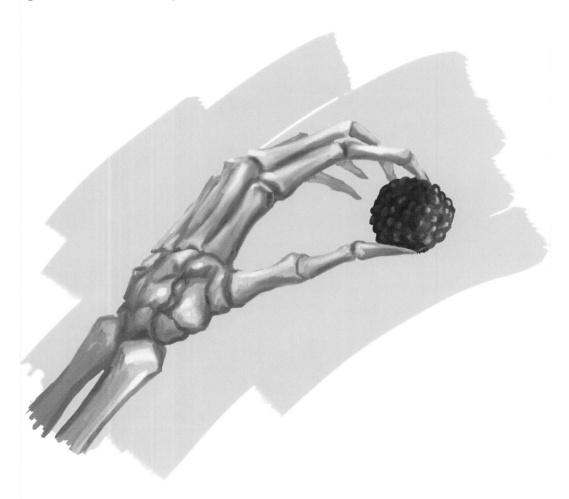

Chiaroscuro

The moment *July* is in the ascendant,
an assortment of sky-lit tenants
needs to be hypnotised by the heat.

In the iced blues of January,
south-facing windows permit slanting sun
to investigate much closer to the ground….
It alights on every cheekbone and pin.

Walking south-east along a three o'clock street,
those who once longed for the prime red-yellows of July
are quite astounded at themselves – at how soundly they are absorbed
into that shadow play, that chiaroscuro.

About Jenny Johnson

JENNY JOHNSON was born in Bristol, England, just after the 1939-45 World War and attended The Red Maids' School – now Redmaids' High School. She began writing poems at the age of five and her adolescent attempts were published in school magazines. As an adult, she joined Bristol Arts' Centre's poetry group, which was run by Bill Pickard. He encouraged her to share her work and submit it to his magazine *The Circle In The Square*. It was in this group that Jenny met the poet Fred Beake, who has taken an interest in her creations ever since. Her poems have appeared in many magazines, journals and anthologies and she has had several collections published, including *The Wisdom Tree* (University of Salzburg) and *Selected Poems: Revised & New* (Brimstone Press). She lives with her husband Noel Harrower in Exmouth, Devon, and has one son.

Photograph by Rob Masding, based on a portrait by Naa Ahinee Mensah

Acknowledgements

Some of these poems have been published in
Anthology of Poems for GreenSpirits, Dream Catcher,
The Journal, Orbis, Poetry Salzburg Review, Sarasvati and *Stand*

The poem *Finding My Bearings* was short listed
in the Buzzwords Poetry Competition, 2020